ELEMENTAL

a memoir

ELEMENTAL

Bill Brown

THREE: A TAOS PRESS

Copyright © 2014 by Bill Brown
All rights reserved

First U.S. edition 2014

No part of this book may be used or reproduced in any form by any means, electronic or mechanical, including photo-copying, recording, or any information storage and retrieval system, without prior written permission from the author, artist, galleries, museums, estates, and publishers.

Book Design & Typesetting: Lesley Cox,
FEEL Design Associates, Taos, NM
Press Logo Design: William Watson, Castro Watson,
New York, NY
Front Cover Photograph: Geraint Smith

Text Typeset in Stempel Schneidler and Avant Garde Gothic

Printed in the USA by Cottrell Printing Company

ISBN: 978-0-9847925-6-6

THREE: A TAOS PRESS
P.O. Box 370627
Denver, CO 80237
www.3taospress.com

10 9 8 7 6 5 4 3 2 1

For John Edgerton, who died in November 2013.
I shared many of the poems in this collection with John,
and I deeply miss his courage, friendship,
and gentle wisdom.

For Suzanne, my truest and best reader,
on the page and in life.

table of contents

The Way	15
The Light That Follows Rivers	17
The Bells	18
Flying	19
Elemental	20
Off Shore	22
Petals, Thorns, Sky	23
This Need	24
Boy And The Poem	25
The Neighborhood Of Air	26
Savor	28
Rare	29
The Peasant Woman With My Father's Hands	30
It Ends And Begins	31
Singularities	32
After Raking	33
First Frost	34
The Fall	35
The Cord	36
Mauve	38
My Wife's Tattoo	39

A Word Growing In Silence	40
Rearview	41
Dark Matter's Love Poem	42
Shelter	44
Winter Solstice	45
What Holds Us	46
Little Statue	48
Someplace Else	50
The Melting	52
Saint Stranger	54
Goldfinch In Spring	55
Magic	56
Rootstock	57
March Eulogy	58
Lent, 2013	60
Tonight Wind Traps Me With Its Sound	62
Habits	64
Applesauce	66
April's Fool	67
Tortoise Morning	68
Late Night, Early Morning	69

How We Become	70
Simple Things	72
For Now	74
Another October	75
Ash	76
Our Death	78
Even As I Dream	80
Winter Harvest	81
Start With A Bad Memory—	82
Winter Still	84
Something Like Grace	86
Coda	89
Driving the County	91
In Appreciation	93
Bill and Suzanne, Mid-1980s	95
Acknowledgments	97
About The Author	99
About The Artist	101

ELEMENTAL

*And does the father who lives in your dreams
Die again when you awaken?*

—PABLO NERUDA

the way

As you start to walk out on the way, the way appears.
—RUMI

The path that led to your childhood creek
was always new. A rabbit, a tortoise, a ribbon snake—
your direction altered by wonder.
There was no test on where you ended up.
It wasn't about how to climb a tree,
but which tree looked lonely without you—
the maple with fall red leaves,
the natural ladder of magnolia limbs,
the creek birch where hummingbirds waited.
The child inside amazed, unstructured time
a blessing—you're lost already if you
always know your destination. Pick a day
when rain dots a window, clouds hug treetops,
a day when you'd like to carry a blanket
over your shoulders like a boy playing Superman.
Let the cat out, let yourself out, time doesn't wait
like a set clock. Bless the porch rocker that rocks
empty in a storm. Bless the armrests that invite
small hands to grip cracked paint, bless the worn
and faded, how comfort comes with old things.
Bless a journey without legs; no need to stand
when eyes walk the forest edge. Bless shadows
trees make when sunlight breaks through
rain clouds. Bless the small accidents of the world—
the barn mow hole weathered into a crooked smile.
Bless the barred owl that lives in the rafters,
and the nightly journey of hunger and death
when its way appears.

the light that follows rivers

Like the light that follows rivers in the night,
    a figure hovers ghostlike in my dreams,
my father or stranger, sometimes the same,
    his blue eyes stained, his thoughts to read.

His gruff hands hover luminous in my dreams,
    above my childhood slumber they touch my head.
His blue eyes like his hands I wish to read—
    yet I am older than my father when he died.

Above my childhood slumber they touch my head—
    his eyes, his hands, his storied voice, all lullabies.
Though I am older than my father when he died,
    as men we travel alone, I know that now.

His eyes, his hands, his storied voice, his lullabies,
    my father, my stranger, always the same—
As men we travel lonely, I know that now,
    like the light that follows rivers in my dreams.

the bells

    Small bells toll childhood's wooden chimes—
        my father's humble laughter,
            the clink of bottles left by milkmen—
                all in another century.
Yet dogs still bark at strangers,
    cats yowl in the thicket
        and mockingbirds defend
            their plots with stolen syllables.
At my age, what isn't stolen?
    Sixty years of keepsakes
        archived in the heart's hockshop.
            Closed during the day,
it opens at night—
    but nothing's for sale,
        just a gallery of faces, places,
            lost emotions wound
into stories—
    how myth invades
        our private lives—
            the rough fingers
of a father's gentle touch,
    a mother's honest demands
        for honest deeds,
            flash of guilt—
has something broken?
    My boyhood friend
        pulls his jeep
            on a gravel road
and we piss the beer
    my brother bought us—
        my friend dead
            these many years,
his face bright, his future
    all his parents wanted,
        this presence in my dream,
        a momentary joy.

flying

We boarded the john boat to explore
the myriad collage of river—light, water,
wind, birds, smell of dead fish, and broken
mussel shells, their mother of pearl
bejeweled along the river's edge.

Great stone bluffs above the far shore held
my grandmother's stories of caves,
rattlesnakes, and the dead—always the dead—
and how the bluffs were willed to spirits
that chose to stay. This is what my thoughts
turned to—mysteries that shaped questions
a boy might ask: Why would hunters
take refuge in a cave filled with serpents?
Why would Indians chase a young woman
off a cliff? And what if a boy staring down
from the high bluff leapt from his brother's arms
and for a moment knew what the woman knew
before she was broken on the rocky shore?

Perhaps that night a tolerant God let him
dream of flying, even soaring above trees
to reach the sun, before the quick heart-
fall into, not the river, nor the shore,
but the cabin floor beneath the bunk bed,
his knees scraped, cheeks bruised blue,
his pulse too desperate for words.

elemental

I.
On the Tellico River, rocks that shape
the water's flow grow smooth and undercut
by this myriad force. At night, shadowed
by sycamore and birch, wherever current
brushes stone, shivers a glow. Light
from distant stars and our squat moon shimmers
Bald River Falls, perhaps tricks natural
selection and our mammalian optic nerve
to accept this magic as just an evening
beside a mountain stream the Cherokee
claim as holy.

II.
Memory changes the narrative:
my grandmother teaching me
how to tight-line fish without a cork.
It's in the feel of the pole, the line tension—
what's in the water on the other end,
the slight lift of wrist when the jerk comes,
all with early willow green, how it can't
be separated in the moment—the elements—
stone outcrop, light in trees, the river—
how an old woman made of flesh commands
such resolve—flesh, mostly water, mineral—
light and shadow, brushstrokes in the eyes,
nuance of voice. My father loved rivers
as much as Jesus—the Buffalo, the Duck,
the Caney Fork, the Tennessee, time there,
earthly sacraments of something he knew eternal.
Why so much hoodoo about heaven
when the river and this life demand our praise?

III.
River, how rain pocks your moving surface—
little rings swirling just enough to confuse
the clouds as tall reeds at your bank form
green sleeves. And how polished rocks
beneath the shoals sing for you.
My wife cracks the window, and your
breeze-song enters sleep like camphor,
as if night holds seashells to our ears.
You are blind to what my eyes gather
from your surface, and yet I use
the second person as if you understand
my syllabic babble. But you speak a language
old as stone. I sit on your bank and glimpse
the everlasting, as a moon rises red
through dark limbs, turns yellow, and brightens
eddy and current swirl—a moon you draw
water from, its lunar drift in every pail.

off shore

Remember how Mother asked our father
to kill a water moccasin at the edge
of Reelfoot Lake? Cautious and deliberate,
with reasons he couldn't deny, though
he hated death, had seen too much of it,
at home and on a battleship in the Pacific.
He didn't care to kill anything;
the snake wasn't intruding, living
its life in its home. But he fashioned
a large stick into a club, then bludgeoned
the serpent that coiled on a log. Night
masked his face—the night I came to recognize.
Why couldn't we move the picnic,
my sister asked, but the deed was done,
and the snake flung like a chain
into open water beyond cypress knees.
We built a fire to appease the gods.
Hotdogs and buns lay in their packages
as evening closed tight around
our tiny spot on the planet, closed
like a constrictor. The sounds
of frogs and night birds rose
against something just off shore
that in years to come resembled
my father's face.

petals, thorns, sky

The crimson petals
   with their velvet touch
      and sweetness
bruise so easily—
   it's the thorns
      that scar.
As a child weeding
   Mother's garden,
      I was warned of rose stems.
A boy who couldn't wait
   for a story to end
      pressed a thorn
against his thumb
   until a blood bead
      ripened.
Who was that boy
   envying mountain
      peaks that tear the sky?
Would there be dreams
   without tearing
      or the sky
that hunkers our shoulders
   toward the earth
      as we age?
The sky—
   the depth of childhood—
      the rose,
   somewhere
      in-between,
         proud thorns
that welcome
   a boy's
      blood.

this need

Don't rush time, Mother said,
it'll come soon enough
and too soon be forgotten.

So I shouldn't write about October
in September, but a needed rain moved
in last night, and today it's 58 degrees
instead of 90. Somewhere in the blood
a need emerges—call it
an unscratched itch, a farmer sitting
on porch steps staring at the sky,
a car waiting for the last ferry.

When I was 13, throwing
the Memphis paper at dawn,
I watched a naked girl run
from a house. A sudden desire rushed
feelings until she turned
and I saw that she was troubled—
running from something—and I felt
ashamed that my selfish passion
was born from her misfortune.

What brought this memory 50 years
later is as unclear as this need—
half orgasmic, half confessional,
a sinner's wish to be holy and the other
way around, an urge to turn down
an untraveled road. An orphan who
dreams he has a mother knows,
even as he dreams, it isn't true.

boy and the poem

Like memory left by a dream
in the mind of a boy, the poem begins.
He shares it with his sister at breakfast—
their dead father by the Elk River.

Later, he tells a friend on the school bus,
finding a better beginning—the campfire,
the green willows at first light.
A clear thread emerges though

the ending still waits in a fog.
Dream sleeps beneath the surface
of his day, awakes in science class
when the teacher's waving arm

reminds the boy of his father's
fly rod whipping the bright air
to place the nymph by a log,
and the explosion as a rainbow

tail-walks, spits the fly
and disappears. Nothing is
finished, not just yet—there is
no consolation until the boy

remembers his father's eyes.
The dream, like the poem,
resurrects the dead, lives
best in the telling.

the neighborhood of air

The start and close of each day
seek silence—first-light's crimson
caressing trees, a dark porch

before locking up for sleep.
The neighborhood of air, a cairn—
moments, like stones, stacked one

on the other to build a monument
to nuance, the numinous, the now.
Dear Self, accept this advice—

nothingness is a diligent mentor;
listen as you feel blood pulse
your temple. Stay tuned to the present's

dotted-line. Pay homage to nourishment,
watch phoebes teach their fledglings
at forest edge—catch gnats for the young,

then disappear in the oak crown
to watch them hunt on their own.
Parents coddle runts, but only for a time.

Deeper in the forest common miracles
occur—wood poppies emerge as if spirits
scatter sun petals. It's dear

to remember how your brother taught
you the flowers' names, how your father
taught him. Whom you teach is not tosh—

being human means more than survival.
You can dress in sack-cloth and dream
you sleep in silk pajamas. Our planet

circles a star. Praise shadows. Sit under
a shade tree, hold out your hands,
and let them spot your fingers.

Imagine light without them.

savor

We have a soul at times...
—WISTAWA SZYMBORSKA

which means at times we don't.
We weave our lives at times;
at times our lives are woven for us.

    Not woolen threads as our mothers
might have it, or cotton, but rayon,
unborn, electric, sticking to our flesh like August.

    Not August gold with drought-burned
corn, but glass and concrete angling the sky
away from grass and bone.

At times a soul claims us
like a lake claims the moon,
wobbles it, stretches it—
God's lamp,

    lighting our names toward home—
my father's supper whistle that brought us
racing behind our spaniel, Wags—the smell
of fresh soup permeating our back porch
like marrow.

We knew even then
the delight hunger makes when sated,
how the soul chooses hunger
over plenty
    because plenty has
so little to follow, and our bread
sopped the last rich savor before
we pled for more.

rare

Even in a world where silence is rare,
I come to this bridge to hear creek water

drift through a line of sycamores.
I kneel beside the oldest tree, where

life has carved a dark hollow the length
of its trunk, listen to wind whistle

its death like a flute, and watch branches,
great white hands fingering the sky.

Fiddleheads cling to roots that reach
in the creek, forming little caves for perch.

A lover of trees, my mother stopped the car
near sycamores to study the strange art

of splotched bark, as if each tree might map
some distant universe. Overhead, a heron

floats to fish the evening shift, drifts without
moving wing to the limestone shore.

I place my hand inside the hollow, rub the scars—
I know something is eating us all, come to love

the dark gnawing and the power it brings.
Too late for shadows, the sun fallen

behind ridge, world itself becomes shadow,
enough to silence the kingfisher and send

her toward home, sound of creek searching
rock and eddy, silhouette of limbs

scratching an evening sky, enough
to send me on my slow walk home as well.

the peasant woman
with my father's hands

After a painting by Jean-Francois Raffaelli

Your eyes, meek and forlorn, will not look
my way, but your hands see everywhere
as they perch in your soiled lap. Fingers
are eyes of sorts. I would reach in the painting

and take them as if they were Father's.
Your nails chipped from labor, dark stains
tattoo your skin like a coal miner's,
like my father's, from handling engine oil

and hot metal. Creases in your palms
spread up thumbs and forefingers, mapping
your life line, a swollen cartography.
Your rough-hewn knuckles are scabrous

but not unbeautiful. I think about the miracle
of the hand bones: radius, ulna, carpals,
meta-carpals, phalanges, dressed in tissue
dense with nerves, designed to pick up

a grain of sand, bludgeon an oak post
with a maul, monitor a fevered brow. *To touch*:
an infinitive that means to cheat, to heal,
to love. It's baffling to think how many hands

I've touched in sixty-two years, and it might be
naïve to consider what a handshake once meant.
But my father reached out his hands to strangers,
tuned cars, swept walks, tied sailor's knots,

taught boys, worshipped girls, cleaned fish,
tethered horses, maneuvered boats, and mixed
the perfect pancake. And I know for certain
a peasant woman's hands in a painting can touch.

it ends and begins

Every morning a story ends,
meadowlark rocking a limb
with its call.

Another begins,
redwing blackbird
with its crimson and yellow
corporal stripes,

or wedding rice
on country church steps,
rain-soaked.

You know them
when you see them—
coyote dance,
abandoned road,
tortoise shell,

child's bonnet on scarecrow,
broken song out car window,
breeze through horsehair-
tattered fence.

It comes when wasp bodies,
dry and severed,
sift windowsills
forgetful as rain sorrow.

It is as righteous
as a virgin's pajamas
on a clothesline,
or the cries that children
save for swings.

singularities

The holy singularities of this now uncommon day...
—C. K. WILLIAMS

While we were gone, the October garden sprouted
ghost stalks and frost-scorched vines—
the neighbor cast bruised tomatoes
across the road to feed the hog. Migrant doves
gleaned the vestiges of corn and beans,

a season's vestments to thatch winter soil.
It is human to make a fall day sacrament—
even rot and decay, the god of entropy,
earth tilting as it parades around a star—
all reasons to worship—if you're warm,

fed and know a dry place to sleep and read.
A flock of waxwings come to harvest
juniper berries, drink in unison
at the metal pot. Their cricket voices season the air.
I have searched for you, even as you shred

hornet's nest and plant fiber, churned with dye,
to make textured paper—how you lose
yourself to discover something new.
On this uncommon day, three Sandhill cranes
stop to rest upon crown above the orchard.

Your green eyes follow their shadows
as you tuck blond curls behind your ear, trailing
a crimson stain on your neck. Winter's knife
is rusty, yet to be whetted by ice and wind,
but something's always coming at fall's end.

So I sharpen its blade with memory—
how I kissed my father's forehead in that
sudden death room, how I held Mother's
small hands, how I woke in an old motel
on a mountain morning to caress you.

after raking

The scent of leaves—maple, oak, gum,
as distinct as vanilla—in early November,
a small rain opens it for all who breathe.

Each raked pile awaits the wheelbarrow
to truck it to the forest edge. Night comes
early—you pray a wind-rise doesn't

bruise your labor. You cover a few piles,
lay the wide rake atop another, a mock effort—
how habits become sacrament in sixty years.

Memory is scattered with raking—
a boy barely taller than the handle,
blistered palms, the joy of rolling

in leaf crunch with spaniel and sister.
How simple work weaves a fabric:
Our mother stood on the porch drawing us

to fresh-baked bread and butter;
father home, late from work, walked
the clean yard in the dark, smiling,

a little jealous of our labor. I stroll
the woods today where frost brings
winter's scent. The last leaves

wave in oak crowns. A few will hang on
'til March when some ancient miracle
of maple roots resumes streaming.

Hepatica and bloodroot will rise
from leaf mold to blossom, catch
sunlight in skeleton of limbs.

first frost

For Suzanne

Grief begins to fade, a sweater
one saves from Goodwill, so
when the first frost announces
fall, you take it from the closet,

an old friend to hold you
as a mother might.
The white rose you planted
for her memory is in full bloom

at October's edge, and mauve,
her favorite color, still lines
the horizon at sunset like it did
in June when you cast

her ashes in the ocean
as night blossomed a froth
of stars. So early evening
we shiver gladly on the porch

with wine, a candle, and
listen to Ella sing *Laura*.
I look at my old guitar,
still cased, something kept near,

that I love to hold in my arms
like you. Rose petals drift
to the floor, and the last finch
flits from the feeder to seek

its roost. A breeze fingers
a familiar tune on wind chimes.
A sickle moon at forest edge
can't harvest the farthest stars.

the fall

In the next room, my wife sleeps soundly,
her even breaths blow against the sheet
pulled over her head as though her mother
isn't lost in a nursing home, as though
mini strokes and diapers do not exist,

as though there is a cure for old age,
for late stage dementia, and our dreams
birth us anew into a clean, clear morning,
like Eve and Adam, sexless, a desire
only for crisp air and the evening shade.

Don't wake her, something says, as I
check to see if the coffee is ready, prolong
her sleep, and for a time the world is motherless
with no serpent under no apple tree,
and the garden is no gated community

in which people who desire knowledge
don't get locked out. But the phone rings,
and the nurse on duty says that her mother
has fallen onto the inflated mattress beside
her bed and doesn't seem to be bruised

or scratched, just fallen like the rest of us
when we wake, like my wife falls awake
in the same world in which she fell asleep
to hear about her mother's fall, not
the first fall, but always the fall.

the cord

        I wake to find you fetal,
smooth skin of thighs,
round hips, knees folded
against your chest. How
we close into ourselves
so naturally when left
to a sleep cycle that quiets
our pulse closer to death—
breathing slow and steady,
anonymous form of prayer,
amnesia of the soul,
the purest voice.

              And I think
of the old man in the alley
behind my school, locked
in a fetal position inside
his cardboard womb, mother-
less, perhaps dreaming
a land of milk and honey
instead of a winter heart,
his thick beard against
his chest, the warmest spot.

   I cover you
to appease the ghost of what
I can't change and turn
away to imitate your posture,
close in on myself, breathe long
and easy before getting up to turn
on coffee, morning chores
ahead, frost covering the pasture,
steam rising from the muzzles
of neighbors' horses—somewhere
the heart's fetus kicks, life cord
spiraling from its stomach,
lost in sleep.

mauve

For Jenny

The silence beneath our words
is often defining, perhaps what
color means in music. Mauve,
your mother's favorite,
a complexity hard to lift
from a palette, shade only
the sky can truly paint.
So say *mauve* and a silence
reaches your mother's dementia.

Her two paintings emerge—
one of a Vermont sunset,
the other, Gulf surf just before dark.
They hang in our house, old friends
that never quite reached her un-
reachable goal—a farmhouse
surrounded by Green Mountains
and the last shade on the horizon
glossing a roll of waves.

I pray your mother dreams
mauve until the sky liberates her
from the nursing home,
lifts her spirit up and we can
cast her ashes out to sea.

And so the word *mauve*, spoken,
becomes an old lady strapped in a bed,
becomes two paintings, becomes
prayer, and a word that must be
said to complete the silence.

my wife's tattoo

It's the Japanese symbol for heron,
needled into her inside wrist, that

most delicate of skin—a place some
people slit, but for her, an ancient bird

that stalks the shallows, its stillness
and shape, the envy of art.

I have watched them wade creek current,
stalk a Gulf beach at mid-night,

and once at Reelfoot Lake, a great blue
caught a snake that coiled the heron's neck

to keep from being swallowed. They
battled for an hour until, exhausted,

both released. My wife says that on a day
when self is unconscious of self,

a heron's sudden appearance in a setting
invades like a memory, unresolved.

It must be studied until a stabbing beak breaks
the water's surface with sometimes an answer.

a word growing in silence

The world is immense
and like a word that is still growing in the silence.
—RILKE

Silence

hovers over the river at dawn—still trapped
in phonemes yet to form, sound struggling
into meaning, into utterance. It drifts just
above the surface of the water as waves,
like a dream, wash tracks from the shore,
tracks like the braille Helen Keller first
realized could form words on fingertips—
wet, cold, hurt, warm, love.

As the first glow emerges in the east, geese
break silence, break formation, splay feet
and splash the surface, erase the easy float
of cirrus clouds that dance with the light.
Morning, you say, pulling sheets from
your shoulder, your eyes still adrift like
the easy lap of water—*morning.*

rearview

Sometimes he looks in the rearview mirror
and sees the old cat standing at the mailbox

with his wife—the cat that stays after it dies,
the wife who doesn't age, her blond curls draping

her chin like soft curtains, as she sits
on the porch steps smiling at the grand

pumpkin she grew that won second prize
at the fair. The straps of her worn overalls

hug her shoulders the way he wished
his arms could drape around her neck, nose

buried in the hair next to her ear, her smell,
orchard fresh, peach or apple or plum.

He loved the way she yelled *look* the time
she pointed at Sandhill cranes circling

the hill above the house and landed, but
he was watching her dance like a ballerina

in garden shorts, hands reaching
at the sky. Now the past circles like ancient

birds and never quite lands where expected,
the orchard dozed by the next owner,

top of the hill a white barn instead
of a pasture crown. A blue pickup emerges

in the mirror, the driver raises two fingers
from the steering wheel, passes on the right.

dark matter's love poem

    Outside locusts chirr,
a thousand tiny engines.
The air itself would plug
its ears if it had the will
to pull empty hands
from its pockets.

    A golden sun lounges
on the horizon and disappears
before anyone gathers it
into the egg basket.

    The magic hen that laid it
rushes the universe edge
toward somethingness.

    Tonight, air is filled
with a veil of dark matter
the atom smasher can't find.

    Even American toads
have ceased their mating calls,
and barred owl is holding
court at the forest edge.

It's a night when every
sentence should start with *hark*,
and an oracle should step forward
and say the news is grief-filled
and good people suffer and die.

As the sky slumbers,
I am glad you stay so close;
even if I can't see your face,
I feel your breath rising
in your chest, and if I still
my heart, I can hear you dream.

shelter

Nothing left of that house but memory anyway.
—MARK DOTY

He's driven past it many times in 40 years—
painted peach one year, antique white a decade later,
same Victorian three-story, new black trim
and porch with rockers. Maples and elms
still shade the driveway. He doesn't know

if day lilies divide the back yard above the creek,
if other boys' play has storied the shadows
with different wars, how adult cares shape make-
believe—games of fallout shelter in the basement.
Because he thought all families ate white beans

on Saturdays, the ham hock meat stripped
and saved for his father, because his world
was filled with snakes, frogs, and roly-polies
instead of television, he didn't know that while
he slept his parents sat at the kitchen table

staring at a checkbook that never balanced.
Whose sister read in silence at her bedroom window?
Whose brother fed a pet crow until a neighbor
poisoned it? Which child fell asleep
on the top step, waiting, waiting?

Now, shadows of strangers stain curtains.
Oh, The Places You'll Go he reads to his grandson.
Who owns a house anyway, after the walls collapse,
the plaster worn into the earth, nothing but
a stone foundation nestled in the grass?

winter solstice

This is the morning we dreamed of—
how night danced to find dawn's
looming light frosting oak crowns,

elf hats of junipers, how out
the bedroom window nothing answers
whispers of crows. Your soft

skin's aglow, a mummy awaiting
her first cup of coffee in bed before
words invade a lexicon of breathing.

It enters my mind how I promised
champagne the next time we made love.
After all, we were just newlyweds

forty-three years ago, lost in each other,
living on bean soup, potatoes, and poetry,
able to scrounge enough change to buy

two Friday night beers. This morning
blond curls still tangle your pillow,
your skin, a salve, to warm cold hands.

December's old man struggles to touch
his toes. Outside, crows still whisper.
Earth knows the shortest day is near.

what holds us

What holds us together
might be memory, selective
images—Green Mountains
where the big malamute

found you on The Long Trail,
her scarf tied by the previous
master—dog that tolerated me
because I was yours too. Or

the little farm house, our first,
with its hill, orchard, and creek
where you found rattlesnake bones
to make jewelry your friends

were too frightened to wear. Or
our work and how its silence
has come to hold us—our
minds and hands busy alone—

mine wording a page, yours shaping
texture and form—two birds in flight,
each choreographing a dance
to accommodate the other towards

a roost, night coming always
and too soon. 6 a.m.: the cats visit
us in bed, *wake up, lazy bones,*
but it is winter and we are nestled

together—my head above the sheet,
a pillow on my chest to block
morning sun—yours covered like
a mummy, a fetus, warm soft skin

under the cloak of self. You mumble
the words a dream awakens.
Do you speak to the dead—
my mother, your mother? How

loss resurrects loved ones, rolls
the stone away—the joy waking
savors and soon fades like the scent
of baking bread, the taste of salt.

little statue

I stare down the trail of childhood
until my eyes blur in the alley behind
Curry Funeral Home where I threw
gravel at crows and stray dogs,
sang the latest song my sister taught,
and tried to imitate my father's
shower tenor. My eyes clear, and I
spy the dead cat in the privet hedge,
its stomach alive with maggots.

   I poke and prod
with a stick until I see infested organs
riddled with motion, its own little universe
of death, alive with other living,
busy before the frost claims it.

   Grasp this trail
for a time, pity the boy lost to all
but memory, the old house empty, no one
home—you're too late to visit. But
wait—when you pulled your socks
on this morning there was a scar
where a boy almost chopped his toe
off with his brother's scout axe.

             December's early
darkness leads the path away
from the kitchen table and a half glass
of cabernet to the mirror a night
window makes. In it a man,
early sixties, has his mother's
brown eyes.

             Little statue,
his beard turning white, lines
in his smile shadowed, haunted
with the boy's old face, still poking
the universe with a stick.

someplace else

This morning the car is a prayer room
in which all mirrors look backwards.
He's written this poem before—
his father's broken smile in the rear-
view mirror, how a child can catch
a glance not meant for sight, or
the one about God in the backseat
counting red barns—and when he
asks *are we there yet,* you know
God means something else.
The older a man gets, he knows
we never get there, and it's alright.

You know the one about returning
to the place from which you started,
but that's not what he means, so
he'll leave that to Eliot. It's more
about the spider on the dash that webbed
its way from the window shade.
The spider has lived in the car for days,
but he doesn't know how—it just
goes about a spider's business
in the place it finds itself.

He wonders about people who dump
old couches on the side of highways.
He spies a yellow one with flowers
and has a mind to pull over and sit,
watch intermittent Sunday morning
traffic. The spider with its hairy
legs and multi-eyed head wraps a fly.
He ponders this development—
with God in the backseat and a spider
on the dash, perhaps humans are
the only creatures who'd rather be
someplace else.

the melting

When someone leaves,
for a long time emptiness
appears in the places
she used to go alone—
by the night window,
or on the porch steps
with the cat—you could
almost speak to it as if
it were her—the emptiness.

What she did in public
can be forgotten, but not
the song she sang raking
leaves and pulling weeds
in the garden.

You will always remember
her hands—small birds
splashing in rain puddles
as she read or told a story.

At some point the absence
dissipates, becomes the posture
of a woman in a restaurant
or stopping at a crosswalk, how
her toboggan hat bleeds curls.

A little farther along,
her laugh isn't right;
even in dreams she acts
strange, won't coddle
your memory—

as if she would erase
herself from your past,
melt like a late March snowman,
eyes and nose just pebbles
in the drive, the stick
arms, windfalls from
a winter storm.

saint stranger

The hill above the orchard is a place
to sit and watch smoke drift

from farmhouse chimneys:
a place where the stranger inside

is welcome. He might speak if
asked, say something nonsensical

and profound as prayer—
I'm here, Lord, not waiting,

no expectations, forget the writing
on the wall. I'll just count crows

and hum with wind in grass.
He's thankful for moments un-

scrutinized—the turkey buzzard
circling the forest edge, his closest

companion, broken world
bandaged for a silent time.

He teaches me to hold out my hand,
and with index finger, write words against

the sky—*I miss the smell of Mother's*
bread, scars on Father's hands, laughter

of a lost friend. Bird whispers
in the brush signal waxwings,

a moment stretched by recognition—
the sweetest God.

goldfinch in spring

Why wish to outlive
              loneliness—
without it, the morning sun
                    would dim,
the goldfinch at the feeder
                would remind
you of no one—a lover would still
                        be gone
these waning winter months.
                    But without her favorite
bird to remind you,
            her absence
would deepen.
          The brightness
of the yellow breast and black cap
                        would stutter
a moment on the optic nerve,
            leave no song
to prick the old mammalian brain
                  like a rose thorn—
the memory of her hair on your cheek,
                    for instance.
Your heart rate would remain
                a pulse driven solely
by the need to arrange
                a hunger without desire,
like some cynical poetry
              that considers a finch
in a love poem
          sentimental,
too soft with feathers
            and its shrill call
untranslatable.
            But the bird's sharp beak
cracks heart-stone seeds
              with such grace.

magic

I remember the sun rising like Lazarus—
dead so long, shocked by its own brightness.
I am thinking about the crow in its maple
at road's edge, how he greets me
when I pass, how he curses each blessed
day with his raucous praise.

My boyhood friend lies emaciated and dying;
there have been times when death stayed mute,
the news blotted out by choice. This morning
crow whispers with the wind, and the hooded
shadow invades a day as ordinary as a dying star
or a fist-size muscle stopping.

As teens, we visited a fortune teller to find out
whom to love. Today the Tarot shadows
the kitchen table, but the wands can't trump
the last card. Our past invades like a beggar,
tin cup outstretched.

Memory returns to Reelfoot Lake
when a storm forced us to wade the snake-ridden
swamp and drag the john boat to Green Island.
A twister formed a water spout of tangled trees.
Ship burned a leech off my ankle with
his cigarette. He always saved my ass
from something, even if he had to conjure it.

Today Magic can't pull a rabbit from a hat
or raise the dead. Nothing rises but the yard crow
and the past, and I bless the stars for both.

rootstock

Her iris in fall sprouts spring
beginnings, kitten ears,
before winter kills.

My mother, diagnosed
with terminal bone cancer,
became angry at first,
her smile dry and bruised.
Then she reached into eighty-four
years of cooking, planting,
pruning, teaching, bird-watching

(at the window
    a notebook for
        species and dates).

She came to accept her fate,
bought her oldest son
a brass candlestick
for the coming night,
shared tacos with granddaughters,
and began to grow again,
to comfort and instruct
with flawless reason and care

 (before the certain
    nosebleeds, seizure-wracking
    headaches, the morphine drip,
    living death that scars
    the living).

Still she left us grocery sacks
of her favorite rootstock—
Cherokee Ridge, Endura,
Daughter of Stars, Adobe
Rose, Come-What-May.

march eulogy

Today heaven is a carless
 country road—
  crow and stray dog,
   resident angels.
They leave the gate
 unguarded—
  no one wants in.
   Cloudy March,
trapped between
 winter and spring,
  wills its inheritance
   to destiny,
and I'm just a speck
 thankful for breath.
  On this side
   of hope—
distant train whistle,
 field of broken thistle,
  toss of broom sage,
   beauty not worth
the penny copper
 of its mane.
  Today anger isn't
   interested,
hangs in the closet,
 pressed and white,
  a Sunday
   shirt.

Lord of sorrow,
    lord of loss—
        my boyhood friend dead,
            his eyes harvested
so someone else
    can see the sky,
        the glint of river.
            Lord of joy, lord of
unmarketable
    small wonders—
        welcome his ashes,
            welcome his ashes.

lent, 2013

I.

A student's poem reads—
born a bastard, her father gone,
she always falls for bastards,
but not again, never again.

A dead friend's ashes inside
black and pewter urn,
free of suffering—his eyes
donated so the blind might see
again a river's moonlit glint.

Crow perched on the Lent Cross
beside a country church doesn't
think herself a symbol.

II.

And there you have it—

A woman's
 will to change,

sixty-five years
 of life reduced and spread
  among forest loam
   to help spring beauties grow,

passing moment
 out a car window
  on a country road.

Woman, man, crow,
 and the world exists.

III.

This morning an ashen sky,
bastard wind shifting oak crowns,
distant crow call, common as rain.
Centuries pass, and still Jesus walks
the streets toward a garden night
and a cup he must drink.

tonight the wind traps me with its sound

    Eaves creak,
        twigs bat the windows,
a long soft howl builds inside.
        Love, stay sound in your slumber
and let me bear alone
        the timbre of coming rain,
how first drops
        against the window
collect and run
        like an old man's tears,
quiet and too dear to wipe away.

        A neighbor's horse speaks
to the night,
        and story enters
an otherwise threadless dark—
        memory, coin purse of moments,
loosens its clasp.
        A brother appears
and Nell, his mare
        with an infected shoulder boil.
With such tenderness
        he rubs salve on her running sore.

A mind loses for decades
    events and practices
that were once dear.
    And now, I'm old man nobody
on a sleepless April night,
    thankful for a history,
how joy and sorrow join hands
    like twins on a swing set,
the past's constant sweeping, sweeping.
    Rain ends and begins again.
I hear a horse gallop in the pasture—
    perhaps an equine act of worship.
If not, I'll claim it as my own.

habits

The way she drank tea
at the kitchen table
with Dickinson's poems;
the way she stood at
the window above the sink
when she knew someone
was coming; the way
she checked the mail,
spoke to the mailman,
sorted bills from personal
letters and *Reader's Digest*—

are these ways I find myself
seated with coffee and Yeats;
staring down the driveway;
or sorting wheat from chaff—
hoping to find a letter
from a lost friend, the way
she's been lost these many years.
The way I mimic her habits
the older I become
brings her back for a time—
hum always off-key but
earnest, hands never still
or empty, desire to once
in her lifetime live beside
water—lake, pond, river—
so she could watch red
maples reflect in fall.

Yet, perhaps she knows
goldfinches still call for her
among brittle cone stalks,
crows land on church steeples
to announce matins, and bats
swirl at dusk, whispering prayers
for rain, mosquitoes, and gnats,
bouncing their echolocation
through flight, *a kind of vespers*,
she would have said.

applesauce

The last of the Arkansas Blacks
were too high for deer, and my mother,
visiting, wouldn't have them wasted—
so I climbed a ladder high into branches,
pillowcase in hand, gathered those I could reach
and shook others into soft autumn grass.

                 The sky,
an October blue, pointed toward
shorter days. The fruit weren't pretty—
spotted with cedar rust, wasp cratered.
Her determined hands, as splotched
as fruit, peeled on the porch 'til
they were done. She sliced and boiled
them to mush, added brown sugar,
lemon juice, and my mother's pièce
de résistance, fresh vanilla, to distinguish
hers from all the rest.

                 This spring morning,
despite a light frost, the old tree burns
white with new blossoms. Mother's
smudged canning apron bleached clean
and folded in a drawer, her busy shadow
gone from the kitchen these many months.
No visits left in this life, except her lesson
about waste, the importance of making
much out of little, the memory of a steamed
kitchen scented with vanilla, and one jar
left in the pantry no one will touch.

april's fool

April hitched in like a vagrant in need of a handout,
but instead, under the brim of her straw hat, sparkled

green eyes that made grass jealous, and when she winked,
I was fourteen again lying on my bed creating on the ceiling

our first embrace. Even the storms pouted tantrums,
a whisper of thunder, rain as soft as a colt's ear.

I was a goner. A creek willow with its slender trunk
and graceful limbs, she promised to stay until corn

sprouted and the burble of Honey Run slowed to a trickle.
Goldfinches lounged in the yard eating dandelion seeds

the wind used to decorate her hair. My days got lost
in mockingbird babble while she taught me to read

the Minoan of sycamore bark, to count a star's twinkle
as mortality, to see a field of chicory as the sea.

tortoise morning

Even the poorest thing shines.
—LAYMAN P'ANG

Today my identity will remain as nameless
as the given name of the tortoise grubbing

my garden. Its shell catches the sun,
sends my eyes an orange not quite

any other orange, an orange Gauguin
might have burnished as an idea of beauty.

It holds a piece of lettuce in its mouth
like a geisha's fan and chews slowly,

fanning the zinnias, the little kabuki.
Maple leaves drip from last night's storm,

a type of silence one can hear, like
snowfall in a forest, a silence that

makes you aware of the silence that is.
Even the crow perched on the fence post

whispers to the mustang something
about the way the pasture smells after rain,

words that can only be spoken in crow.
Perhaps being nameless sharpens the senses

when the sun rainbows blades of grass
and morning's an infant too young to speak.

late night, early morning

Through the open window,
    I hear the rain begin, feel
        myself smile in the dark.

Late summer drought has
    grass burnt brown,
        deer sleeping near the river,

and woodpeckers drinking
    hummingbird water.
        We embrace often,

not just desire, but out of
    a need to touch—
        hold on

something says—*hold on*
    to thwart emptiness
        caverned by need for change.

Now large yellow daisies
    will line the creek;
        ironweed will bloom purple

above the fence
    to close the season.
        Spirits lift when color

anoints the landscape.
    Autumn seeks a different numbing—
        some pull in the body needs it,

resignation that resembles hope,
    when new words form a syntax,
        welcoming morning's first chill.

how we become

How we become
    who we become
        is a conundrum,
so many bridges
    crossed over creeks
        with names
we promised
    to remember: Knob Creek
        Cub Creek, Sinking.
Some mornings,
    we rise early,
        names disappearing
from our tongues.
    Heron, osprey,
        brook trout—
first love,
    brother,
        grandmother with cane pole,
can of red wigglers
    we dug beneath
        barn straw;
not stolen
    but mostly lost
        to the insistence
of an adult world
    and its misdirection.

            But the creeks haven't dried up,
their song, a ripple
    over limestone
            older than bone,
memory fading
    and so dear,
            we dare not rush from it.
What's the cost
    if we sacrifice
            sentiment to cynicism?
Drought can't erase
    the scent of
            coming rain.

simple things

There are these simple things—
pile of leaves and sticks to burn,
sky to funnel the smoke, blue

chimney with a hawk being chased
by a smaller bird that pecks
at its tail, and a cow with her calf.

There's a pond turned into a hazel
eye by a grove of cedars covered
in frost. A neighbor boy across

the road tosses a baseball in the air,
hits it, slings the bat and runs
imagined bases, slides into home.

I know he wins. The child in all
of us should hit a home run, hear
the crowd roar. I stand, rake in hand

like a rustic in a painting. I don
my hat for art's sake and point at
something distant, lost in brush

strokes—it's always coming at the edge
of the canvas, out the window
of a vacant house. Old age certainly,

but not that desolate—spirit
of winter maybe, when dusk arrives
at 4:30, then pinks and grays

left by our sun, then night, that
little eternity with moon and stars,
completes itself as morning comes.

for now

                Last night
a dream woke him with the tale
of a boy finding flat stones to cast
upon the lake, how he counted
dotted skips and circles they make.
Today coffee stains mar the words
he awoke to write.

                Let the day's will
have its way with September. Let cats
lie on the porch like sleep addicts, let
raccoons wreck bird feeders, let the yard
fill up with plastic grocery bags
that divide and multiply like cancer cells.
Look on the bright side—the mass of
ragweed will seed for winter cardinals,
and the downy woodpecker has learned
to drink from the hummingbird feeder.

                He'll mobilize—
wade in Sinking Creek, watch the white
heron stalk shallows, cast a rock
for the boy who lurks in birch shadows,
pray a late afternoon storm shares one last
drink with the browning corn.

another october

Morning curls maple leaves, sings with wind chimes
in dogwoods ripe with red berries for winter cardinals.

The birth of something akin to sorrow pans for gold
in Sulphur Creek. Memory sharpens a kitchen knife

for the coming cold. November gives up, but October
meditates, too rich with mantras to follow one.

A house is left open for a stranger who never comes,
because he's here with me—I've borrowed his name.

Each day he drifts with windows, weather, and
a porch for watching seconds pass. Empty spaces

created by tree trunks shape doors when sun separates
shadows. Which one will he finally walk through

to teach me to be more thankful than I am?

ash

After a rainy week, I build a fire
the way Father taught me.
Choose a cloudy day with little wind,

take dry tinder saved to flash a flame.
Crisscross kindling and split logs,
prop a backlog above the ground,

chimney to draft the fire, and burn
ash, hickory, and even bodock.
By choice and need, my father's life

was cluttered by demands. Perhaps this stoked
his love of burning. So I start in early morning,
rake an opening in the yard and light the fire,

by afternoon, two acres clear of old year's tatters—
winter's breakage and windfall limbs gathered,
gardens cleaned of sticks and leaves, ripe for mulch.

To appease the god of tired backs and aching joints,
my wife and I follow Father's ritual—
wrap sweet potatoes and acorn squash in foil,

place lemon, garlic and a chicken in Dutch oven,
then pile coals around. While supper cooks,
we walk the forest edge and find white buds

of bloodroot bursting through hardwood soil,
willing to risk a late frost scorching.
We pour a glass of wine, unwrap our meal,

and say a brief prayer for the man
whose fettered life loved burning,
and burned to ash so soon.

our death

You've been dead
almost as long as you lived,
    and still birds
eat black oil at the feeder,
    the little house
you built when I was twelve.
    Like everything dead,
it is falling apart. Cardinals
    and finches
don't mind. Today, ideas flit
    in and out
like blowing leaves, maple and gum.
    They cover
the ground as I try to pick the one
    I need
to hold me here. I lie in them
    and they crush
beneath my hips—I become a museum
    pharaoh, chin
sticks out, nose points to the sky,
    eyes almost
blind to the circle of buzzards scouting
    for carrion.
Some mornings focus on winter and death—
    no God
would argue with physics, not in the solstice
    month when
shorter days blink by, feed on memories—
    a father dead,
a feeder's decay. Leaves make their own bed,
    and I lie in it.

Today the Goddess of December relies
    on these infant
needs—suck—warmth—touch—always
    touch, as I fondle
dry veins of maple with fingertips,
    my own death
buried beneath me, and daydream how
    your whiskers
rubbed my cheek when I was young.

even as I dream

    you dead,
            your stories witnessed

    at the funeral, cemetery
            tent shading the family

    from bright sun, smell
            of mown grass and fresh dirt,

    the simple pine box you
            requested covered with lilies—

    I awaken to a sun born again,
            and you're still alive

    to visit one more time,
            and even when you die,

    I will dream you living,
            cupping hot tea

    with two hands
            on a winter's day—

    as I have dreamed my father living
            time and time again,

    his unshaven chin
            against mine.

winter harvest

It's a clumsy foundation, how hardwoods support the sky,
the fallen leaves, snow-covered. A kestrel on a power line
rocks raptor thoughts like Father's fingers tap-danced

an armrest. One more morning a dead father's habits haunt,
poignant in winter when mortality flies with falcons
combing the roadside. My closest childhood cousin

died last night. Born two weeks apart, we sailed
the seven seas on our grandparents' porch swing,
searching the floor for buried treasure. Now X marks

the spot where his dust will be posited—his boyhood
wonder and adult sorrow diminished to fragile plight.
What we grieve for a time is buried, dug up later to reveal

who we become. Today I am numb, blanketed by snow,
sky a bland gray, the only green, hooded junipers
brushing horizon, its canvas blank, the day's palette

without paint. Metaphor and her tired comparisons
fumble, inscrutable as sycamore bark. Sycamore limbs,
those brittle fingers, strain to hold up the sky.

Grief will soon strain as well to gather lost moments
like a farmer gathers peaches until his harvest
must be divided to keep from bruising fruit.

start with a bad memory—

      your father's dead blue eyes
          stare at the ceiling,
the doctor hovers over him,
      stethoscope probing his chest
          like a vacuum cleaner,
but there's nothing left
    to retrieve except
        spittle on his chin.

Now, a few questions—
    Why write poems thirty years
        later about this same event?
Death has enough power.
    Why not remember
        the bonfire builder,
man at whose feet
    dogs worshipped,
      the shower
 resounding his tenor,
   I'll fly away in the morning,
       tenderness of his callused hands?

And your mother's screams—
    crying out to God—
        let's say they were operatic,
mythic—Leda, for instance, or Icarus;
    Prometheus and his liver ailment
        for sneaking fire to man.

Now picture a fire grate
    in the upstairs
        bedroom,
    how the night before his death
        they held hands
and poked socked feet
    through flannel pajamas,
        blue coals sparkling their eyes.

winter still

All we have left is the astronomy of Hope.
—RICHARD JACKSON

Stark limbs above ground-fog
turn the ridge into a giant skeleton
when first light brushes hardwoods.
A dream lingers at heart's edge,
wordless, haze like a snake's eyes
just before it sheds its skin, a blindness
before the metaphor for renewal begins
about spring. But it is winter still,
and the news which knows no season
is layered with fresh bodies, the missing
child's corpse found in a basement,
jaw bone of a girl washed up
on a Caribbean shore. There's the story
about World War II soldiers digging
a trench in France, uncovering bones
of World War I soldiers—earth's
graveyard grows, folds in on itself.

The music I recognize this morning
is the towhee's ground-feeding call
echoed by its mate—all to the acoustic
background of wind in dead beech leaves.
Become wordless long enough to listen,
learn the behaviors of animals and plants,
a kind of trance, dreamlike, that depends
on beauty of language to calm the brute.
Believe in the ways of death, how nature
will wear you away like beetle grubs
do tree bark. But this poem isn't supposed
to be about entropy, or snake skin,
or a girl's jaw scattered in sand.

This poem wants to get back to the dream—
towhee grubbing winter ground to survive
until spring—or even to an orphaned child
in war rubble who finds a can of C-rations,
peaches in thick sauce, opens it
with scrap of tin, drinks the nectar down.

something like grace

I was taught that God dwelled close
enough to drag my open fingers
through the air of Him,
particles adrift with holy energy
blessing the hearts of hungry
children and demented souls
in nursing homes—praise them.

I was taught to pray for my enemies—
terrorists, bigots, bullies, and investors
who grow rich off the working poor—
praise them.

And especially praise be to columbine,
and iris which return in my garden
each spring like miracles, nudged
with 10-10-10 that dissolves into moist soil,
brought by sacred rain—praise them.

And children's small hands, busy
in wonder of their senses—may
they investigate all that doesn't harm—
may tiny creatures they study live
without injury.

Thanks be to April and October
for birthing what I love and
to January and August for teaching
me to tolerate what I don't.

Creator of small industries—
ants trucking leaf bits toward holes,
bees dancing honeysuckle maps,
homeless collecting aluminum cans
from roadside ditches—praise them,
praise them all.

And praise to dark matter that holds
the universe together and tears apart—
and to night windows, first light
and clumsy hands that reach
beyond themselves.

CODA

driving the county

Today the road leads beside Cross Creek,
where shade from fall leaves,
maple and sycamore,

blinks light on water and stone,
as the sun spins earth on its journey,
and dark matter swells cosmic gravity—

always in flux like fields of starlings
combing for seeds amidst broom sage
and timothy. An ancient mound rises

above Indian Grave Point Cave,
entry to the afterlife in another time.
This earthy swell, worn by centuries,

is part of the mystery our footsteps tread
before they are blown clean or washed
in the creek with its burble and light.

The word *Father* emerges in prayer,
habit learned in childhood, my father
dead some 47 years, just a pinch of sand

in the desert. Time, like the energy
in matter, drags creation forward.
I could say *Mother* instead, and another

constellation is lit—say *sister*, say *brother*,
say *wife*, say *work*, and the circle
of a man's life from birth to now

appears like asters in late fall,
vibrant as a brushstroke of purple
to dapple the autumn swell.

in appreciation

My deepest thanks to Larry Richman and Jeff Hardin for their brilliance and friendship.

Working with Andrea Watson of 3: A Taos Press has been a pleasure. Her sharp insight and amazing energy make her an excellent editor and publisher. Thanks, as well, to Madelyn Garner for her poetic skills and suggestions.

I thank *Still: The Journal* for nominating "Our Death" for *Best of the Net Anthology*.

I celebrate Margret Renkl, Chapter 16, and the work they do for writers and writing in our region.

I greatly appreciate Humanities Tennessee, The Tennessee Arts Commission, and the Downtown Nashville Public Library.

Bethel College, Bread Loaf School of English, Radford University, and Vanderbilt University—your influence and heart still inspire me. MTSU Writer's Loft, thanks for keeping me in the poetry game as a mentor. Tennessee Mountain Writers and Iris Press, you truly have been a powerful force in my life.

Bless Sue Orr for Learning Events and the work she does for writers in our region.

Bless my brothers and sisters for continued love and support.

BILL AND SUZANNE, MID-1980s

acknowledgments

Grateful acknowledgment is made to editors of the following publications in which some of these poems first appeared, sometimes in different forms:

Aurorean:	Another October
Big Muddy:	April's Fool
Borderlands: Texas Poetry Review:	Magic
Cloud Bank:	Applesauce
Conclave: A Journal of Character:	Saint Stranger
Crab Creek Review:	Goldfinch In Spring
Dos Passos Review:	Rearview
Hamilton Stone Review:	Little Statue
Howl:	Even As I Dream
Main Street Rag:	Someplace Else
Maypop:	The Peasant Woman With My Father's Hands
Number One:	A Word Growing In Silence, Ash, For Now, Her Iris, Need, Rare, The Fall
Poem:	Driving the County, Singularities
Potomac Review:	Mauve
Raven Chronicles:	Elemental
Red Rock Review:	Off Shore
2nd & Church:	How We Become, Simple Things
Still: The Journal:	Our Death, Start With A Bad Memory, The Light that Follows Rivers
Southern Humanities Review:	My Wife's Tattoo
Tar River Poetry:	The Way, Tortoise Morning
The Broad River Review:	Boy And The Poem, Flying, Late Night, Early Morning, Savor, Shelter
Versal:	Habits

about the author

Bill Brown, who grew up in Dyersburg, Tennessee, is the author of six collections of poetry, three chapbooks, and a writing textbook on which he collaborated with Malcolm Glass. During the past twenty years, he has published hundreds of poems and articles in college journals, magazines, and anthologies. In 1999, Brown wrote and co-produced the Instructional Television Series, *Student Centered Learning*, for Nashville Public Television. He holds a degree in history from Bethel College and graduate degrees in English from the Bread Loaf School of English, Middlebury College, and George Peabody College. Since 1983, Brown has directed the writing program at Hume-Fogg Academic High School in Nashville. He retired from Hume-Fogg in May, 2003 and accepted a part-time lecturer's position at Peabody College, of Vanderbilt University. In 1995, the National Foundation for Advancement in the Arts named him Distinguished Teacher in the Arts. He has been a Scholar in Poetry at the Bread Loaf Writers Conference, a Fellow at the Virginia Center for the Creative Arts, and a two-time recipient of fellowships in poetry from the Tennessee Arts Commission. In 2011, the Tennessee Writers Alliance awarded Brown Writer of the Year. He and his wife Suzanne live in the hills of Robertson County with a tribe of cats.

about the artist

Geraint Smith was born in a small mining town in Wales. He moved to Pasadena, California, and subsequently to Taos, New Mexico, in 1988 after numerous trips photographing in the Southwest of the United States. Smith continues to live and work in Taos where he opened the Geraint Smith Gallery of Fine Art Photography, showcasing his landscape and wildlife images. He conducts *Land of Light Personalized Photo Tours* and operates three-day *Taos Photo Safaris and Workshops* from his gallery.